# Interactions

W9-AUQ-073

By

**Debbie Pincus**

**Illustrated by**

**Heidi Stetson**

Cover by Vanessa Filkins

Copyright © Good Apple, Inc., 1988

ISBN No. 0-86653-448-2

Printing No. 9876

**GOOD APPLE, INC.**
**BOX 299**
**CARTHAGE, IL 62321**

# Dedication

Dedicated to the memory of my dad, William Pincus, my fiancé, Mark Lasky, and my dear friend Laura Penn-Bourget, who always helped me get along.

To those with whom I share special relationships, who gave me their listening ears, honest feedback, valuable insights and constant support. Thank you, Dr. Norman Brier, Reva Pincus, Mitchell Milch, Arlyne Eisberg, Achim Votsmeier, Lil and Sol Lasky.

# About the Author

Debbie Pincus is the Director of Counseling at the College of Mount Saint Vincent and a psychotherapist in private practice in New York City. She designed and implemented the Interpersonal Communications Program in many public and private schools. Ms. Pincus leads workshops and seminars on effective communication, which have received national recognition, and she was selected for inclusion in *Who's Who Among American Human Service Professionals*. She is the author of the book, *Sharing*, published by Good Apple, Inc., in 1983.

# About the Illustrator

Heidi Stetson is a cartoonist/illustrator living in western Massachusetts. She is the creator of the United Features Syndicate comic strip *Ophelia and Jake*, and has contributed illustrations to several publications, including *The Christian Science Monitor* and the *Boston Phoenix*. Other work has included advertising illustration and greeting card design.

# Table of Contents

# Introduction

Getting along with others requires patience, tolerance, acceptance, love and understanding of oneself and others. It also takes the development of interpersonal skills which first must be learned and practiced.

*Interactions* is a workbook that offers students a fun, nonthreatening and creative way to become masterful at interacting effectively and a success in interpersonal relations. The activities help students develop the ability to get close to others while maintaining their own uniqueness and individuality.

The book is divided into five chapters: Me, Myself and Others; Actions, Reactions and Interactions; Getting Along with Anger; Cooperation and Competition; The ABC's to Solving Problems. On the back of each activity page there is important information for the teacher. Each home project page should be torn out and taken home to be worked on as homework with the family. The activity is a follow-up and reinforcement of the topic discussed and the activity completed in class. Information for the parents is on the front of each home project page.

## Note to Students

Each activity in this workbook is intended to further your individual development as well as develop your capacity to get along with others. The more successful you are in personal relationships, the more self-confident you will become. The more self-love and joy you experience, the more self-esteem you will possess. Have fun with each activity and share your knowledge with your family. They may want to join in the fun and learning.

## Note to Teachers

The back of each activity page provides you with the objectives of each activity as well as background information for yourself and the students. It also gives you questions to ask students in class discussions and ideas for effectively teaching the lesson. An activity should not be started by students until a class discussion of the topic takes place and directions are given.

## Note to Parents

Your child can master the skill of getting along with practice, reinforcement, discussion, and with your support. Take a few minutes each day to listen and take interest in what he is learning by participating in his home project activity. Your relationship with your child will improve and so might your own interpersonal skills!

# Me, Myself and Others

Who you are and how you feel about yourself has a lot to do with your relationships with others. The activities in this chapter will increase your understanding of yourself and the significant people in your life.

### Before You Begin "Me, Myself and Others"

Paste pictures of yourself and the people who mean a lot to you in the frame below.

# Words, Words and More Words

Complete the crossword puzzle. If you have difficulty, use your dictionary. When you succeed, consider yourself a master of *relationship* vocabulary! You will also understand the meanings of words used in this chapter and throughout the book. Have fun!

## Across

1. working together
2. connection between two or more things
3. to frighten
4. to respond to something
5. support, help
6. close, familiar

## Down

1. a contest or match of skill or ability
2. to act on each other
3. a part of something; something added to form a mixture
4. necessity
5. worth
6. to reply; answer

## Words to Be Used in the Puzzles

| | | | |
|---|---|---|---|
| intimate | intimidate | relationship | cooperation |
| need | competition | interact | depend |
| value | react | respond | ingredient |

# For the Teacher

**Purpose:** To help students improve their vocabulary and understand the terms used throughout the book.

**Process:** Teach students how to use a dictionary and ask them to look up any word listed on the bottom of the page that they do not know the meaning. Discuss the words and their definitions. Also teach students how to do a crossword puzzle.

Have the students answer and discuss the following question:

● Does the meaning of any word in the puzzle bring to mind a:

> thought
> feeling
> memory
> image
> response
> idea

If so and if willing, share it through a picture, sculpture, poem, dance or writing with your teacher and classmates.

**Answer to the puzzle:**

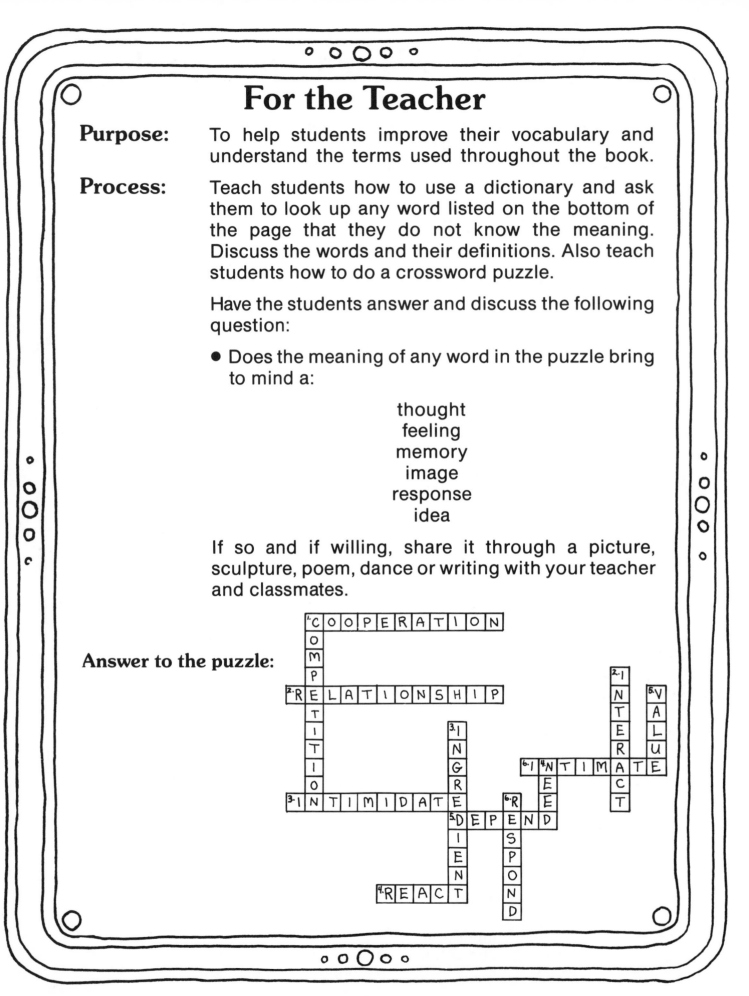

# For the Parents

Word, Words and More Words is an activity that will help develop your child's vocabulary while giving him a chance to express thoughts and feelings about his family. Listen as he reads his story aloud. Accept whatever thoughts and feelings your child expresses rather than judge, question, interrogate or dismiss. You may want to write your own story using the words listed to share with your child.

# Words, Words and More Words
# Home Project

Write a story about you and your family. The only rule is that you must use six of the twelve words from the crossword puzzle (they are listed below) in your story. Read your story to at least one family member.

INTIMATE                   COOPERATION
NEED                           DEPEND
VALUE                        INGREDIENT
INTIMIDATE            RELATIONSHIP
COMPETITION        INTERACT
REACT                       RESPOND

# Signature Bingo

**Directions:** Get signatures of people in your life that fit the descriptions below.

**To Win:** Get five signatures across or four signatures up and down.

**Prize:** Having many important people in your life!

| | | | | |
|---|---|---|---|---|
| A person you respect very much.<br><br>Tell the person why you respect him.<br><br>_____ | A person you can always depend upon.<br><br>Let this person know how you depend on him.<br><br>_____ | A person your feelings have changed for.<br><br>Tell him how they've changed and why.<br><br>_____ | A person who would come to you with his problems.<br><br>Tell the person how this makes you feel.<br><br>_____ | A person you like to model yourself after.<br><br>Tell the person your reasons.<br><br>_____ |
| A person you feel very comfortable being with.<br><br>Tell the person what you find comfortable about him.<br><br>_____ | A person you enjoy competing with.<br><br>Challenge this person to something.<br><br>_____ | **FREE**<br>Find someone who _____<br>_____<br>_____ | A person you feel most similar to.<br><br>Share your similarities and differences.<br><br>_____ | A person who knows you better than anyone else.<br><br>Find out something new about him.<br><br>_____ |
| A friend that you've known the longest.<br><br>Share some early memories.<br><br>_____ | A person you enjoy laughing with.<br><br>Share a funny joke and spend some time laughing together.<br><br>_____ | A person who intimidates you.<br><br>Tell him your reasons and feelings.<br><br>_____ | A person you have very little in common with and admire.<br><br>Find some commonalities.<br><br>_____ | A person you'd go to for an opinion.<br>Ask this person for an opinion about something. Agree or disagree with him.<br><br>_____ |
| A person you fight the most with.<br><br>Tell the person appreciations and resentments you feel for him.<br><br>_____ | A person that makes you feel special.<br><br>Let him know how he's special to you.<br><br>_____ | A person you would share your deepest secret with.<br><br>Share one with him.<br><br>_____ | A person who often makes you angry.<br><br>Tell the person those things that make you angry.<br><br>_____ | A person you enjoy being silly with.<br><br>Be silly together.<br><br>_____ |

Discuss with your teacher and classmates how you feel, knowing that you depend on others and others depend on you.

# For the Teacher

**Purposes:** To help students identify important people in their lives; for each student to appreciate his signficance to himself and others.

**Process:** Tell the students that they have as long as they need to complete Signature Bingo. It is not a contest between students but rather a chance for each student to be a winner. Suggest that when they complete the activity they announce this to the class and share any thoughts or feelings about their process in getting Bingo. For those who have not completed Bingo after a few weeks, encourage them to finish the activity.

Have students answer and discuss the following questions:

- What is important to you about depending on others?

- What is important to you about being depended on?

- What do you find difficult about making friends? Keeping friends?

- What do you notice about the special qualities of the people most important to you?

# For the Parents

In order for a child's self-esteem to develop, he must feel that he matters to others and others matter to him. Signature Bingo gives your child the opportunity to acknowledge those who help shape his personality and give meaning to his life. In recognizing the importance others have on him, your child will feel more secure. Spend some time "bowling" together. Try to knock all the pins down.

# Signature Bingo
# Home Project

Once you have completed the task written in a bowling pin, ask a family member to write his signature over it. See if you can get a strike by getting a signature across every pin!

Tell each family member his importance to you.

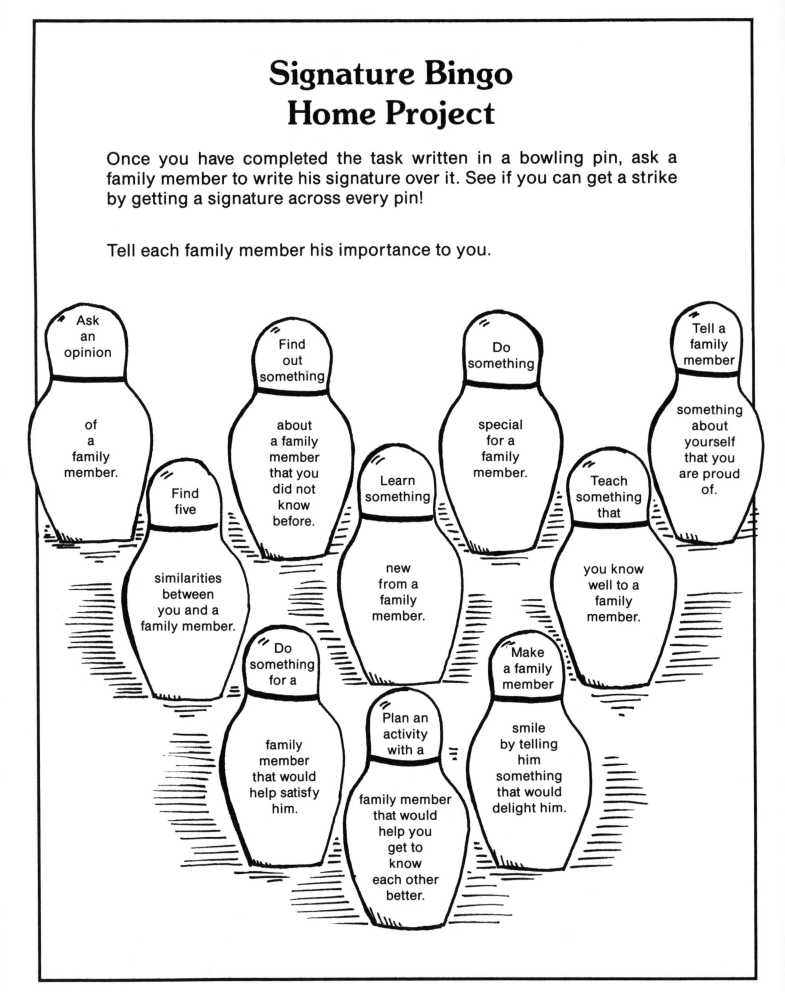

**Ask an opinion** of a family member.

**Find five** similarities between you and a family member.

**Find out something** about a family member that you did not know before.

**Learn something** new from a family member.

**Do something for a** family member that would help satisfy him.

**Plan an activity with a** family member that would help you get to know each other better.

**Do something** special for a family member.

**Make a family member** smile by telling him something that would delight him.

**Teach something that** you know well to a family member.

**Tell a family member** something about yourself that you are proud of.

# Relationship Recipe Cookbook

Cook up Relationship Recipes by deciding the ingredients necessary to create the following items on the menu. Use the words on the side of the page and the examples below to help you.

Be sure to add your own words to the lists on the left.

POWER
PRESTIGE
KINDNESS
HUMOR
STRENGTH
HONESTY
APPRECIATION
CARING
SENSITIVITY
LOYALTY
WEALTH
INTELLIGENCE
AFFECTION
SINCERITY
LOVE
MORALS
DEDICATION
DEVOTION

**RECIPE WORDS**
CUT
DIP
WHISK
SPRINKLE
DASH
COMBINE
GARNISH
SQUEEZE
MASH
POUR
BAKE
TOSS
MIX
BEAT

**Example:**

### FRIENDSHIP

MIX:
3 tablespoons of kindness

ADD:
1 cup of sensitivity
2 teaspoons of understanding
a dash of humor
sprinkle in honesty

**MENU**

trust
friendship
respect
care

---

Sue knows that she can tell Carol a secret and Carol will not gossip. She *trusts* her.

### TRUST RECIPE

Bob would drop almost anything to help his friend Jason. Bob and Jason have a strong *friendship*.

### FRIENDSHIP RECIPE

Jennifer values Nora's ideas, thoughts and opinions. She has a lot of *respect* for Nora.

### RESPECT RECIPE

Dan has a great deal of concern for his younger brother Todd. Dan *cares* about his brother.

### CARE RECIPE

Discuss with your teacher and classmates the ingredients you value in your relationships.

# For the Teacher

**Purposes:** To help students develop awareness of the qualities that are the foundations of relationships; to encourage evaluation of their relationships.

**Process:** Have students share situations in their lives that demonstrate *trust, friendship, respect, care*. Then ask them to formulate definitions for each word.

Ask them to rank the ingredients as to their importance in order to determine proper measurements for each.

These recipes, when completed, can be compiled into one large booklet and distributed to each class member, or each recipe can be hung on a bulletin board.

Have students answer and discuss the following questions:

- Which ingredients do you most value in your relationships?

- Which ingredients are easiest/hardest for you to offer others? Why?

- Which ingredients are easiest/hardest for you to receive from others? Why?

- Which ingredients are currently missing from your relationships?

  What steps will you take to develop them? List these steps.

# For the Parents

Relationship Recipe Cookbook is a fun way for your child to acknowledge the qualities necessary for building valuable relationships. This activity provides the child with the opportunity to determine the ingredients that nourish him when interacting with the important people in his life.

Cook up your own recipes with your child while discussing the ingredients that would improve your relations with each other.

# Relationship Recipe Cookbook
# Home Project

Write the name of each family member in a box under the column labeled *names*. Then choose at least one box next to each person's name and write about an experience you've shared with that person that demonstrates either *trust, friendship, respect* or *care*.

| NAMES | TRUST | FRIENDSHIP | RESPECT | CARE |
|-------|-------|------------|---------|------|
| Mom | | Mom and I planned my birthday party. | | |
| | | | | |
| | | | | |
| | | | | |
| | | | | |
| | | | | |
| | | | | |
| | | | | |

# Fibs, Truths and Wishes

List the biggest fibs you can think of that would describe how you get along with the people listed below.

## FIBS

Example: (sister) I never once got angry with my sister.

(best friend) _____

(sister) _____

(brother) _____

(parents) _____

(teacher) _____

Now list the truest statements you can think of that would describe how you get along with the people listed below.

## TRUTHS

Example: (sister) I care about my sister very much but sometimes wish she were someone else's sister! I hardly ever talk to her.

(best friend) _____

(sister) _____

(brother) _____

(parents) _____

(teacher) _____

Now list how you wish to get along with the people listed below.

## WISHES

Example: (sister) I wish I could be more patient with my sister.

(best friend) _____

(sister) _____

(brother) _____

(parents) _____

(teacher) _____

Tell each of the people above your wishes.

# For the Teacher

**Purposes:** To help students clarify how they get along with others and how they wish to get along with others; to help students develop the steps necessary to getting along.

**Process:** Begin by asking students to define the words *fibs, truths* and *wishes.* Tell them that sometimes in order to see something that is very true, we need to look at its opposite, something that is absolutely false. And by looking at the way something actually *is* (the truth), we can see if it is OK or not OK with us. If it is not OK with us, we can decide our wish that would make it OK. Then we can determine the steps necessary to make the wish come true. Tell students to let their imaginations run while writing their fibs and to spend some serious thinking time when determining their truths and wishes. Encourage them to share their wishes with the people involved.

Have the students answer and discuss the following questions:

- Who do you get along best with? What helps you get along so well?

- Who do you have difficulty getting along with? What keeps you from getting along with each other?
(envy, competition, dislike, differences?)

- If someone asked you the secrets of getting along well with others, what would you tell him?

# For the Parents

Fibs, Truths and Wishes helps your child take a closer look at how he gets along with others and a chance to decide how to improve the interactions that are not OK with him.

Listen as your child verbalizes his wishes for change, and help him determine the steps that will possibly make his wishes come true.

Share some of your own Fibs, Truths and Wishes with your child.

# Fibs, Truths and Wishes
# Home Project

Read aloud your fibs, truths and wishes to a family member. Ask him to try and guess which are the fibs, which are the truths and which are the wishes. Then discuss with him the steps below.

**Wish #1** _____

         Steps 1 _____
               2 _____
               3 _____
               4 _____
               5 _____

**Wish #2** _____

         Steps 1 _____
               2 _____
               3 _____
               4 _____
               5 _____

**Wish #3** _____

         Steps 1 _____
               2 _____
               3 _____
               4 _____
               5 _____

**Wish #4** _____

         Steps 1 _____
               2 _____
               3 _____
               4 _____
               5 _____

**Wish #5** _____

         Steps 1 _____
               2 _____
               3 _____
               4 _____
               5 _____

# Actions, Reactions and Interactions

INDIFFERENT   MISCHIEVOUS   SMUG   JEALOUS   SHEEPISH   CONFIDENT

DEMURE   WITHDRAWN   CURIOUS   UNDECIDED   SYMPATHETIC

AGONIZED

Every action causes a reaction which makes for an interaction. The activities in this chapter will help you understand and improve your interactions by having you closely examine your actions and reactions.

## Before You Begin "Actions, Reactions and Interactions"

See how many of the vocabulary words below you can find in the chapter. Underline the word in red when you find it on a page and circle it in blue when you know its definition. Use the pictures on this page for the activity called "Expressing Yourself."

APOLOGETIC

LONELY

THOUGHTFUL

SUSPICIOUS

MISERABLE

effect
experience
alternative
illustrate
enraged
innocent
indifferent
optimistic
paranoid
perplexed
prudish
relieved

dialogue
judgmental
mosaic
agonized
arrogant
blissful
bashful
demure
eavesdropping
exasperated
sheepish
smug

DISBELIEVING

AGGRESSIVE

BLISSFUL   ANXIOUS

HAPPY   DETERMINED

SATISFIED   SHOCKED   ARROGANT   CAUTIOUS   ENRAGED   BORED   HURT

RELIEVED   EAVESDROPPING   BASHFUL   PRUDISH   EXASPERATED   FRIGHTENED   GUILTY

PERPLEXED   DISAPPOINTED   DISGUSTED   INTERESTED   DISAPPROVING   SAD   FRUSTRATED

# Chain Reaction

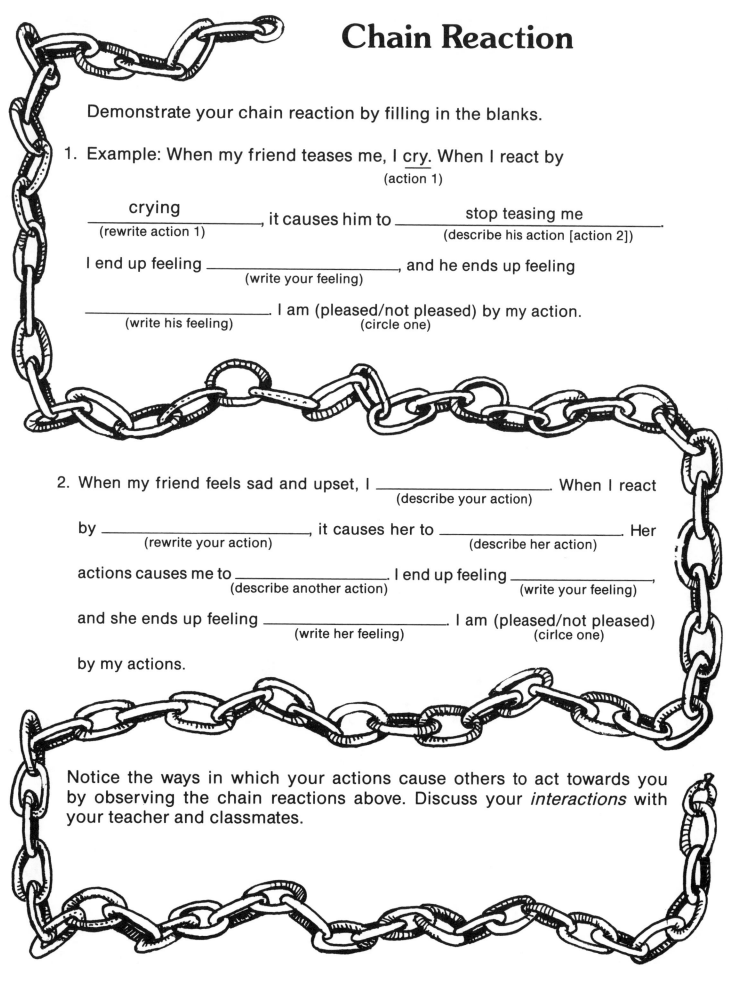

Demonstrate your chain reaction by filling in the blanks.

1. Example: When my friend teases me, I <u>cry</u>. When I react by
                                   (action 1)

   <u>  crying  </u>, it causes him to <u>  stop teasing me  </u>.
   (rewrite action 1)                     (describe his action [action 2])

   I end up feeling _____, and he ends up feeling
                     (write your feeling)

   _____. I am (pleased/not pleased) by my action.
   (write his feeling)                   (circle one)

2. When my friend feels sad and upset, I _____. When I react
                            (describe your action)

   by _____, it causes her to _____. Her
     (rewrite your action)                  (describe her action)

   actions causes me to _____. I end up feeling _____,
             (describe another action)              (write your feeling)

   and she ends up feeling _____. I am (pleased/not pleased)
                     (write her feeling)          (cirlce one)

   by my actions.

Notice the ways in which your actions cause others to act towards you by observing the chain reactions above. Discuss your *interactions* with your teacher and classmates.

21

# For the Teacher

**Purposes:** To help students look closely at their interactions; to heighten student's sensitivity to others by helping them see the effects their actions have on others.

**Process:** Help students to understand "chain reactions" by pointing out how an action causes a reaction and so on and so on. Give them examples of positive and negative chain reactions and help them discover ways to change negative chains into positive ones.

Have students answer and discuss the following questions:

- Which actions of yours caused the other person to react negatively? Positively?

- Which actions of yours caused you to feel bad? Good?

- What actions have to change for you to end up feeling satisfied with your interactions?

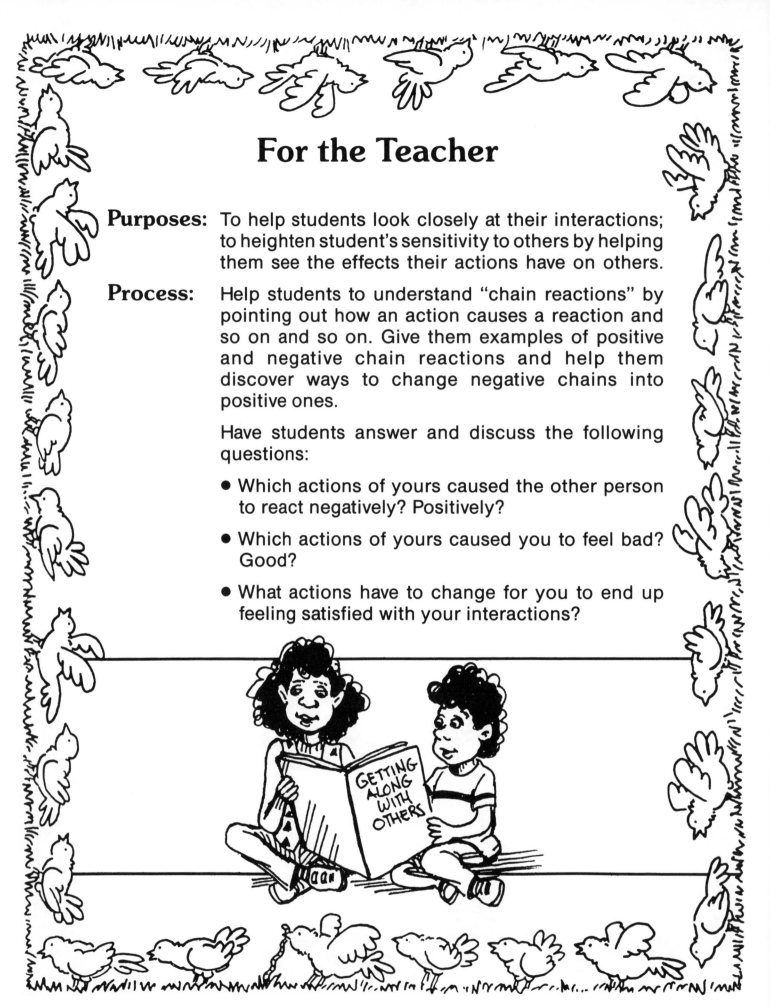

# For the Parents

As your child understands the feelings his actions cause others, he will become more sensitive in his interactions. The Chain Reaction activities are creative ways for your child to take a closer look at the effect his actions have on others and the impact that other people's behavior has on him. Help your child create a CHAIN REACTION family booklet by drawing your own chain reaction cartoon that depicts a typical family scene. Add this to the collection.

# Chain Reaction
# Home Project

Does this sound familiar?

You announce that you don't want to go to the dentist. Your mother gets upset and calls Dad, Dad yells to you that you're going no matter what, you slam your bedroom door causing the cat to jump off the table, in fright, and break your sister's watch causing your sister to push the cat away causing the cat to land in the bushes outside the door causing your brother to laugh causing your baby sister to . . . .

Choose an action of yours that causes a chain reaction in your family. Draw the entire scene in a style similar to the cartoon below. Keep the page as the first of your CHAIN REACTION family booklet to be added to by you and other family members.

*(A) Daughter angry, can't play outside with friends. (B) Mother yells, "Get to room to finish homework." (C) Causes son to get knocked in face. (D) Flies off skateboard. (E) Spills ice water on Dad's bald head. (F) Cat runs and hides . . . .*

# I Did It Because . . . .

Write down how you imagine feeling and acting in the situations listed below. A is an example of possible feelings, actions and reactions that a person might experience. Remember, every person will react in a different way. There is no correct response.

## Situations

A. Classmates tell you that you can't be included in their game during recess.

B. Your brother/sister or parent interrupts you during your favorite TV show and tells you to turn off the television.

C. You notice a group of your friends whispering about you.

## My Feelings
## (because of this situation)

A. hurt; left out; angry

B.

C.

## My Action
## (because of my feeling)

A. I sulk in the corner by myself.

B.

C.

## My Feeling
## (because of my action)

A. lonely; rejected

B.

C.

If you are not satisfied with the feeling you end up with, try to change your action so that you will end up feeling better. List the changes below and discuss them with your teacher and classmates. See how many alternative actions you can come up with.

## Changed Action

A. I tell my classmates that they hurt my feelings and I find someone else to play with.

B.

C.

## Changed Feeling

A. confident; satisfied

B.

C.

25

# For the Teacher

**Purposes:** To continue to increase students' awareness of the cause and effect relationship of feelings and behaviors; to help students discover behaviors that will cause positive feelings for themselves and others.

**Process:** Ask students to think about how they would feel and react to the situations listed. Point out to them the connection between their actions and their feelings. Explain that we often cause ourselves to feel bad feelings because of the behaviors we choose, but we often blame others for making us feel bad. Help students understand that we can't choose our feelings, but we can choose behaviors which affect our feelings. Explain this by discussing alternative ACTIONS and pointing out the changed feelings.

Have students answer and discuss the following questions:

- What are some of your typical reactions to your feelings of anger, sadness, hurt, disappointment, jealousy, fear?

- Do your reactions cause you to feel better or worse? What would you like to change about those reactions? How could you go about changing them?

- What situations seem to make you most angry, sad, pained, lonely, satisfied, happy, interested, frightened, confident?

# For the Parents

I Did It Because . . . . is an activity that will help your child make connections between his behaviors and feelings. He will become aware of the effects of his own actions, begin to take responsibility for them and discover alternative behaviors to those actions that cause negative rather than positive feelings. Hopefully, the words *I Did It Because* will make sense to both you and your child, and satisfying interactions will have taken place.

# I Did It Because . . . .
## Home Project

Write and illustrate your own cartoon strip by following the directions below each box.

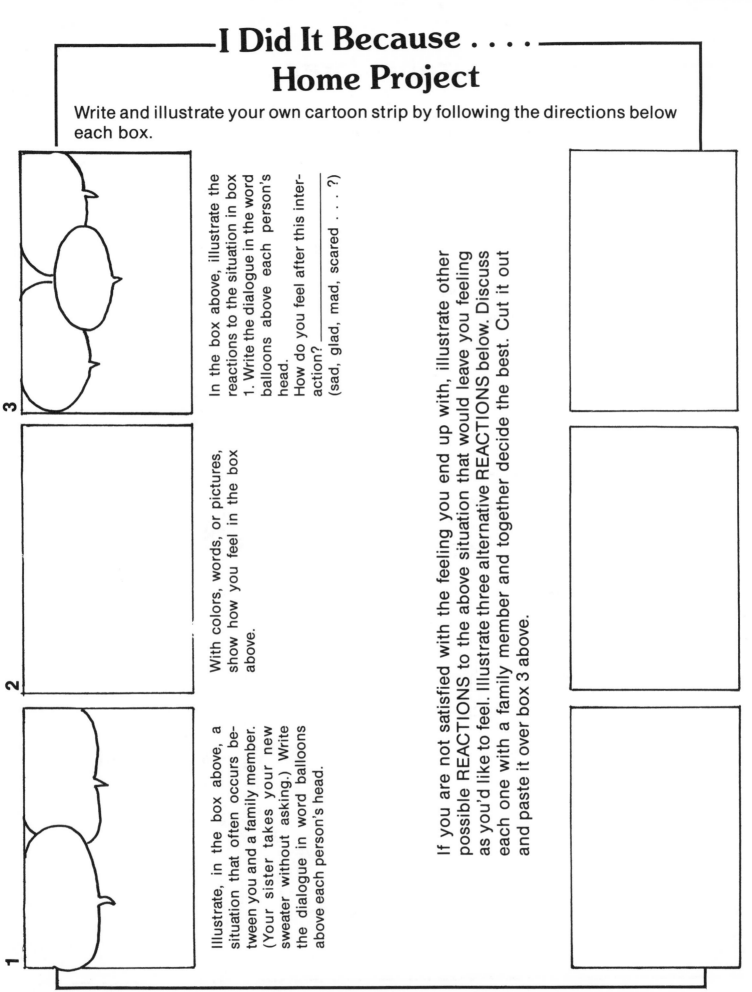

**3**

In the box above, illustrate the reactions to the situation in box 1. Write the dialogue in the word balloons above each person's head.
How do you feel after this interaction? _____
(sad, glad, mad, scared . . . ?)

**2**

With colors, words, or pictures, show how you feel in the box above.

**1**

Illustrate, in the box above, a situation that often occurs between you and a family member. (Your sister takes your new sweater without asking.) Write the dialogue in word balloons above each person's head.

If you are not satisfied with the feeling you end up with, illustrate other possible REACTIONS to the above situation that would leave you feeling as you'd like to feel. Illustrate three alternative REACTIONS below. Discuss each one with a family member and together decide the best. Cut it out and paste it over box 3 above.

# Unfinished Stories

Complete the stories by following the directions below.

1. Add an ending to this story so that the main character ends up feeling PROUD. Put your name or make up a name in the boxes labeled MAIN CHARACTER.

[          ]  forgot to complete his homework.
main character                    her
                              ‾‾‾‾‾‾‾‾
                              circle one

He was nervous and upset because he wanted to get an A in the class, and his teacher and parents would be angry with him. His best friend offered him his homework to copy. _____

_____

_____

_____

_____

_____

_____

_____

_____

2. Add a beginning to this story so that the main character ends up feeling RELIEVED. Put your name in the box labeled MAIN CHARACTER.

_____

_____

_____

_____

_____

_____

_____

_____

[          ]  took a deep breath. He
main character                    She
                              ‾‾‾‾‾‾‾‾
                              circle one

was glad things turned out the way they did, and he ended up feeling confident and relieved!

# For the Teacher

**Purpose:** To develop students' writing abilities while deepening their awareness of cause and effect relationships.

**Process:** Ask students to brainstorm a list, which should be written on the chalkboard, of all the possible actions that the main character in story #1 could take that would leave him feeling proud. Point out how an action leads to a feeling and a feeling leads to an action. Explain that we most often have choices to the ways in which we act and feel and therefore are responsible for our actions. Tell the students to choose an action from the list that would leave the main character feeling proud and write it as a story. Do the same for story #2. The completed stories should be read aloud to the class and discussed.

Have the students answer and discuss the following questions:

- Tell about a time that you took responsibility for your actions. (For example, you chose to walk away from a fight instead of fight.)

- Tell about a time that you took responsibility for the way you felt. (For example, you felt upset that your close friend did not come to your birthday party. Instead of pouting about this, you chose to enjoy the friends that were there. You ended up feeling loved and happy.)

- Why is it important to know your choices before you act?

- Why is it important to take responsibility for your actions and feelings? What happens if you don't?

# For the Parents

Unfinished Stories are thought-provoking activities that will deepen your child's awareness of his interactions with others. He will learn to see the many choices he has regarding his actions and feelings and take responsibility for them. He will understand more fully the consequences of his behavior.

# Unfinished Stories
# Home Project

Describe an interaction that you had with a family member in which one of you ended up feeling CONFIDENT.

_____
_____
_____
_____
_____
_____
_____
_____

Describe an interaction that you had with a family member in which you felt HURT but ended up feeling LOVED.

_____
_____
_____
_____
_____
_____
_____
_____
_____

Describe an interaction that you had with a family member in which you learned something positive about yourself and about the other person.

_____
_____
_____
_____
_____
_____
_____

Read these interactions to family members and share your thoughts and feelings with one another.

# Expressing Yourself

Learn how to express to other people, in a nonblameful way, how their actions make you feel. This will help stop negative chain reactions from occurring.

Cut out and paste in the blank spaces the face and feeling word (found on page 20) that would best describe your feeling in each situation below. Draw a feeling face of your own if none on the page fit.

When you share secrets with others and not me, I feel

When you break dates with me, I feel

When you tease and talk behind other kids' backs, I feel

When you invite me to your house and to your parties, I feel

When you notice the things I say and do, I feel

When you leave for summer vacation with your family, I feel

When you _____, I feel
          write a specific behavior

When you _____, I feel
          write a specific behavior

When you _____, I feel
          write a specific behavior

When you _____, I feel
          write a specific behavior

Now write six "When you . . . , I feel . . . ." statements to the people listed below. Make sure to express these statements to them in a nonjudgmental, caring tone of voice.

When you _____, I feel _____. (to friend)

When you _____, I feel _____. (to parent)

When you _____, I feel _____. (to sibling)

When you _____, I feel _____. (to classmate)

When you _____, I feel _____. (to teacher)

When you _____, I feel _____. (other)

Why do you think that the saying of "When you . . . , I feel . . . ." statements to others helps to stop negative chain reactions from occurring and helps to create positive interactions? Discuss the reasons with your teacher and classmates.

# For the Teacher

**Purposes:** To teach students a new communication skill that will improve their interactions with others and help them identify their own feelings; to increase students' self-esteem by identifying and expressing their feelings in a constructive way.

**Process:** Explain to students that "When you . . . , I feel . . . ." statements are not blameful because the speaker owns his feelings about the other person's specific behavior. Statements that blame and cause negative chain reactions usually begin with YOU (you never give me any of your soda; you are so selfish). Statements which show the person taking responsibility for his feelings and that create positive chain reactions begin with "When you . . . , I feel . . . ." (When you do not share your soda with me, I feel left out.) Discuss with students the differences between the two types of statements and reasons that the latter creates more positive interactions. Also, help students to understand when it is appropriate to express their feelings to others and how doing this will help them to feel better about themselves.

Have students answer and discuss the following questions:

- How do you feel and react when someone blames you?

- How do others feel and react to you when you blame them? What is the interaction that usually follows?

- How does expressing your feelings to someone in a constructive way help you to feel better about yourself? Feel better about the other person? Help them to feel better about you?

# For the Parents

Children need to express their positive and negative feelings to others in a nonblameful way. The Expressing Yourself activity teaches your child a communication skill that will improve his interactions with others and help him to identify his own feelings. When a child learns to identify and express his feelings in a constructive way, he begins to build confidence and relate effectively with others. Get to know your child better by understanding, not judging, his feelings.

# Expressing Yourself
# Home Project

Design the mosaic below. Decide how each situation would make you feel and color that space as the key indicates.

## Key

betrayed = blue
disappointed = green
excited = purple
angry = yellow

scared = light blue
sad = red
happy = orange
jealous = pink

loving = brown
proud = black
confident = light purple
hurt = light green

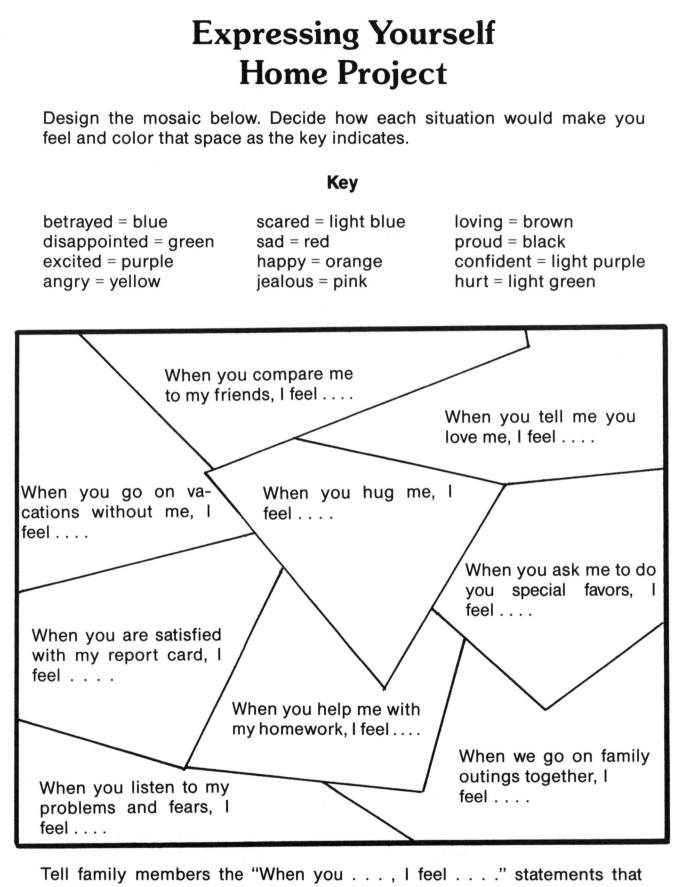

When you compare me to my friends, I feel . . . .

When you tell me you love me, I feel . . . .

When you go on vacations without me, I feel . . . .

When you hug me, I feel . . . .

When you ask me to do you special favors, I feel . . . .

When you are satisfied with my report card, I feel . . . .

When you help me with my homework, I feel . . . .

When we go on family outings together, I feel . . . .

When you listen to my problems and fears, I feel . . . .

Tell family members the "When you . . . , I feel . . . ." statements that are true for you. Share your completed mosaic with them.

# Getting Along with Anger

Anger is a common emotion that you will often experience in your interactions with others. How you handle it will affect your relations with others. The activities in this chapter will give you ideas to effectively handle this powerful emotion.

## Before You Begin "Getting Along with Anger"

Find the vocabulary words hidden in the word maze, circle them and write their definitions below. Have fun!

```
R S U L K M U C O N S E Q U E N C E L P O R
L T U M K C D R U L M M C B D R U T Q U A E
X R E V E N G E M T C D E U W I T H D R A W
A A U J P R O D U C T I V E L Y D U G A D C
M T M C D I S T R A C T Z S L P Q S D A E O
D E F F E C T I V E L Y B O L U O U G I T P
A G M N E D Y N S E N S I T I V E Z N A O E
I Y C R I T I C I Z E A B O J I M I J N R G
E C K O P A L J O Z L T R A N E G E Y O N Y
O U M C K I R A D M U C R E S O L V E J M E
```

Write the definitions below.

sulk _____

effectively _____

strategy _____

consequence _____

revenge _____

criticize _____

withdraw _____

resolve _____

sensitive _____

cope _____

productively _____

distract _____

# Heating Up and Cooling Down

Write situations involving others that cause your temperature to rise. See what makes you explode!

**Examples:**

When my parents raise my sister's allowance and not mine.

When my friends don't help me clean my room after we play. I get stuck doing it myself.

When I don't understand the homework and no one will help me.

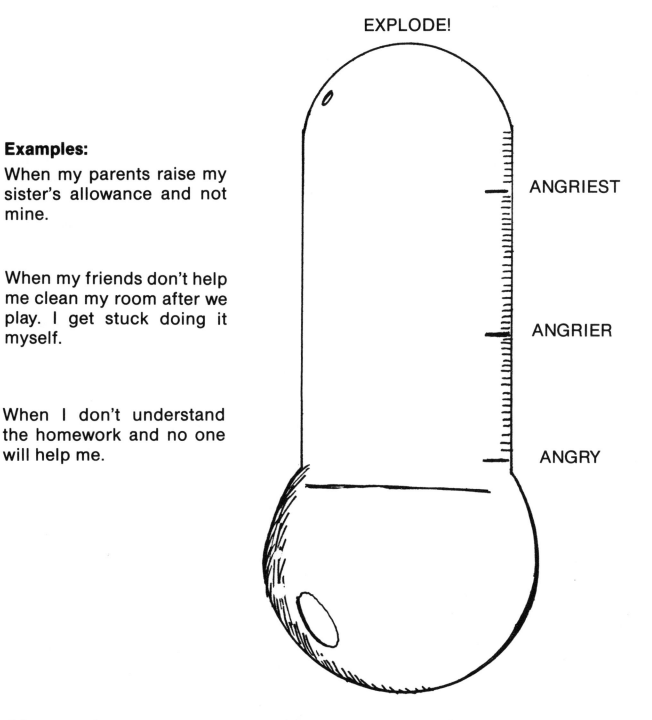

EXPLODE!

ANGRIEST

ANGRIER

ANGRY

Discuss with your teacher and classmates the situations that make you feel angry, angrier and angriest! Mention how you cope with your feelings (sleep, yell, fight, cry, hit others, sulk, discuss).

# For the Teacher

**Purpose:** To help students identify and accept feelings of anger; students will discuss ways they cope with their angry feelings.

**Process:** Explain to students that in any relationship, fights and arguments are unavoidable. Interactions will cause conflicts, misunderstandings, and tensions which will cause fighting and anger. Ask them to think of situations in their own lives that have caused them to feel angry and how they coped with their feelings. List on the board all the coping strategies mentioned. Remind them that feeling or being angry at someone is not good or bad, right or wrong. However, the way a person copes and expresses his feelings of anger can be constructive or destructive and, therefore, can be evaluated. Evaluate together the coping strategies that are listed. Decide the most helpful ones and have students adapt those.

Have the students answer and discuss the following questions:

- Think of five situations that made someone else angry at you. How did you feel with anger directed at you?

- How do you feel directing your anger towards the person causing you the feelings? Is it easier to forgive them and be angry at yourself? Discuss.

- List the five coping strategies that work best for you when you are angry.

  List the best coping strategies when someone is angry at you.

  (Explain that coping strategies are behaviors that help a person deal with a difficult feeling.)

- What is a constructive way to express your anger toward someone? Destructive? Which is easier for you?

- How do you feel about yourself when you are angry?

- What are the advantages to a relationship of expressing your anger? What are the disadvantages?

# For the Parents

Effective interactions usually do not take place while a child is feeling heated. He must learn ways to cool off and calm down before expecting anything constructive to take place. The cooling down process might take minutes, hours, days or weeks. Heating Up and Cooling Down activities will help your child recognize if he is heated up or cooled down and will teach him how to let go of anger and deal with it appropriately. Add your own cooling strategies to the ice cube.

# Heating Up and Cooling Down
# Home Project

Anger cannot be dealt with effectively while you are heated up. What are the ways you can help yourself and others to cool down? Write as many ways as you can think of on this ice cube below. Ask family members for their cooling down strategies when you run out of your own ideas. Cut out your ice cube and look at it when you are seeing red!

exercise

taking a walk

listening to music

# What Would You Do?

Read the story below. Then draw yourself in John's shoes and suggest to him the best way to deal effectively with his angry feelings. Write the letter A, B or C in the word balloon above your head and explain to him why you chose it. Ask your teacher to then read you the results of your choice.

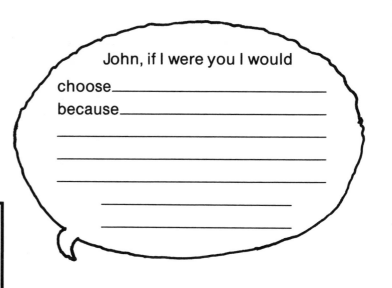

John, if I were you I would

choose_____

because_____

_____

_____

_____

_____

_____

---

The most popular kid in the class, Bill, continually picked on John. But it was true that John had huge feet, skinny legs and couldn't catch a ball to save his life and Bill and his friends got a kick out of teasing him. John felt embarrassed, hurt and most of all ANGRY!

---

What would you do if you were John? Read A, B and C and suggest the one to him that you believe would have the best results. In order to decide, answer the following questions about A, B and C.

In which would John feel good about his behavior?

In which would John end up feeling confident about himself?

In which would John be most effective in stopping the teasing from continuing?

In which would John not hurt others but rather solve the problem?

### A
John was furious. The next day at recess when Bill and his friends called him "knobby knees," he picked up stones and started throwing them at the boys. And then he took the ball they were playing with and threw it at Bill's stomach.

### B
John was furious. He cried to his best friend, Greg, and told him about all his angry and hurt feelings.The next day John pulled Bill aside and told him that his teasing was causing him to feel angry, hurt and embarrassed and that he must stop it. If he didn't, he'd have no choice but to tell their teacher.

### C
John was furious. The next day at recess John called him nasty names and teased him back about his fat legs. This way Bill would know what it felt like.

# For the Teacher

**Purposes:** To help students learn effective ways of dealing with their anger; to increase students' awareness of the consequences of their choices and actions.

**Process:** Explain to students that the emotion of anger is neither right nor wrong; good nor bad. However, the way they choose to express their feelings can be constructive or destructive and therefore can be evaluated. Teach students questions to ask themselves in order to determine if their expression of anger will be constructive or destructive. Then ask the students to read the story and decide which action of John's would have the best results. Point out to them that pretending to put oneself in someone else's shoes helps to deepen sensitivity to another person's feeling and experience. Remind each to draw a picture of himself in the shoes and explain in the word balloon why he chose the alternative that he chose. Remember to read to the students the result of each alternative chosen. They are listed below. Ask them if they are still satisfied with their choices. Discuss the best alternative and why.

Below are some questions that students can ask themselves in order to decide if their expression of anger will have constructive or destructive results. Tell the students to add more of their own questions.

If I express my anger in this certain way, will I end up . . .

- feeling OK about my actions?
- gaining confidence in myself?
- hurting anyone?
- getting in trouble and/or being blamed?
- having more enemies or friends?
- resolving the problem?
- making more problems?

**Result of:**

**Alternative A**
Ms. Smith, John's teacher, came running out to see what the commotion was about. She saw John throwing stones at Bill and had John sent directly to the principal. She comforted Bill and his friends.

**Alternative B**
John felt calmer and less angry after talking to Greg and therefore more able to know what he wanted to say to Bill. Bill was surprised to see John standing up for himself and respected him for it. He also knew John meant business and he'd get in trouble if he continued. Bill told his friends to stop teasing John.

**Alternative C**
Bill was not going to take this kind of name-calling from a wimp like John. He got all the kids against John and gave them orders to tease him as much as possible. Things got worse and worse for John.

Anger is a common emotion children face almost daily and a difficult one for them to cope with. It usually leads to fights and arguments and results in hurt feelings. What Would You Do activities help your child learn alternative ways to deal with anger with results that are constructive, not destructive. Your child will learn to use his anger constructively and interact in a way which allows him and others to feel respect and respected. Write a different middle to the story and share it with your child. Compare results.

# What Would You Do?
# Home Project

Write your own middle to this story. Make sure to read the ending before you begin.

Carol was watching her favorite television show when her brother, Gary, barged in and turned on the baseball game. He said it was the most important game in the series and he HAD to watch it. This happened almost everytime Carol would try to watch TV. Her parents were tired of their fighting. Carol had been warned that the next time they heard them fighting over the TV, neither of them would watch it for a week. Carol did not want this to happen, but she was furious at her brother.

_____

_____

_____

_____

_____

_____

_____

_____

_____

_____

_____

_____

_____

Carol was pleased with herself. They didn't get in trouble and Carol got to watch her favorite program. Best of all, she worked out a plan with her brother that even he liked! She was no longer angry but instead satisfied and proud.

Discuss with your family the strategy you used to help Carol effectively deal with her anger. Discuss reasons why anger is not always easy to deal with when you are in the heat of it.

# I Would Like . . . .

Circle the ways you would like to be treated by others when they are angry with you.

I would like the person to tell me why he's angry and NOT yell at me.

I would like the person to bring up all the things in the past that he's also angry about.

I would like the person to withdraw and refuse to speak.

I would like the person to yell and hit me so I could learn my lesson.

I would like the person to be sensitive to my feelings.

I would like the person to ignore me.

I would like to know exactly what made the person angry with me.

I would like the person to express his anger in a private place where other people can't hear.

I would like the person to give me a chance to speak so that I can also be heard.

I would like the person to criticize me and put me down.

I would like the person to do mean things to me for revenge.

I would like to be forgiven.

I would like to make up after the anger is expressed.

I would like to understand and discuss our differences and plan ways to resolve our conflicts.

Discuss with your teacher and classmates the ways you'd like and not like to be treated when others are angry with you. Tell your reasons. Which are harmful ways to be treated?

# For the Teacher

**Purposes:** To increase sensitivity to the feelings of others when expressing anger; to have students determine if they treat others the way they wish to be treated when angry.

**Process:** Make two columns on the chalkboard which read: Feels OK/Does Not Feel OK. Ask the students to brainstorm a list of ways others have treated them when angry and have them tell if these felt OK or not OK. Discuss the reasons. Then go over the Feels OK list and ask students if they treat others in the ways that feel OK to them. Ask what stops them if they don't. Help students develop the ability to treat others the way they would like to be treated and to be sensitive to how others feel with their expression of anger. Point out the appropriate (not harmful) and inappropriate (harmful) ways one can be treated. (Children that are emotionally or physically abused at home may not know the differences.)

Have students answer and discuss the following questions:

- When someone expresses angry feelings at me, I can handle it if . . . .

- When I'm angry with someone, I can express it best when/if . . . .

- When someone expresses his anger toward you, what is most hurtful? Most helpful? Most frightening?

- When you express your anger at someone, what is Most harmful? Most helpful? Most frightening?

- What would you like to change about the way you treat others? Others treat you?

- What can you do if someone is expressing anger in an inappropriate/harmful way to you?

# For the Parents

Children can develop sensitivity toward others when they examine the ways they would like to be treated themselves. I Would Like . . . . activities offer the opportunity for your child to decide this and will help him determine if he is treating others the way he likes to be treated. Help your child to discover that when anger is dealt with appropriately in relationships, conflicts can be resolved and intimacy can develop.

# I Would Like . . . .
# Home Project

Circle the ways you treat others when you are angry with them. See if they are the same ways you expect and like to be treated when others are angry with you. Look back on your "I Would Like . . . ." activity page.

I am sensitive to the other person's feelings.

I like to make up after I've expressed myself.

I forgive the person after I've expressed myself.

I like to discuss and resolve our conflicts when and if possible.

I speak to the person about my feelings. I do not yell at him.

I give the other person a chance to express his point of view.

I tell the person specific behaviors that made me angry.

I express my anger in a private place where other people cannot hear.

I do not talk behind the person's back. I keep what is between us, between us!

Do you treat others the way you say you like to be treated? Discuss with a family member. Do you treat others in harmful ways when you are angry?

# That's Not Fair!

Make a list of ways you feel you've been unfairly treated. (Do not use names.)

Do not leave anything out! When all your classmates' lists are completed, you'll each take a turn standing on the podium in front of the class for "That's Not Fair!" storytelling. One student will begin by telling his "That's Not Fair!" story. At the end of his story, another student will stand up and say, "You think that's not fair, listen to this one!" The storytelling continues. After everyone has had a chance to tell his most unfair story, you will discuss with your teacher and classmates ways to cope with the unfairness you have experienced and will experience in your life.

It was unfair when _____

_____

It was unfair when _____

_____

It was unfair when _____

_____

It was unfair when _____

_____

_____

It was unfair when _____

_____

_____

It was unfair when _____

_____

It was unfair when _____

_____

Ways to Cope with What I Feel Is Unfair

_____

_____

_____

_____

_____

# For the Teacher

**Purposes:** To give students the opportunity to complain, be listened to and acknowledged in a fun, nonthreatening and supportive way; to learn ways to cope with injustices; to understand that unfairness is a fact of life; to practice and develop oral speaking skills.

**Process:** Begin by teaching students the skills involved in presenting a believable, persuasive and interesting story. Explain that this will make the difference between being and not being listened to, acknowleged and understood. Then set up a podium in front of the class for each student to stand on or behind. Inform students of the rules: one person tells a story at a time with no interrupting. Each person has three minutes. When the teacher gives the signal, in unison, the class says, "You think that's not fair, listen to this one!" When each student has had his turn, form a circle and have the students answer and discuss the following questions:

- How did you feel before complaining? While you were complaining? After complaining?

- Did you feel listened to and supported for your feelings?

- Which ways of coping with unfairness feel most comfortable and positive for you? How do you cope with the unfairnesses in your life?

- Is there really such a thing as fairness? Do you think *expecting* things always to be fair makes sense? Why or why not? Will expecting fairness all the time cause you disappointment, frustration and anger? What is reasonable to expect?

- What can and what can't be changed in your unfair situations? How can you accept what can't be changed?

- Who can you go to, trusting that your "that's not fair" will be listened to, acknowledged and understood?

Remind students that excessive complaining is not productive. Expecting things to always be fair is not realistic and leads to frustration and anger.

We all like and need to complain from time to time about all the injustices we experience. Injustices are a fact of life, since there is no universal "fairness." However, the feeling of being treated unfairly probably is the leading cause of anger, particularly in children. "That's not fair" are probably words you have heard your child cry many times. These cries often get ignored by adults since they either sound petty, adults fear paying attention to them because they believe this will cause more complaining or the adult simply feels helpless in making things better. Actually, when a child is simply listened to and taken seriously, the complaining usually disappears. Often the *real* "that's not fair" underlying all anger is the feeling of not being important enough to be listened to and taken seriously. By simply allowing a time and place for complaints to be voiced, your child will feel supported. If you help your child learn how to productively channel his anger, he will reach many of his desired goals in life.

# That's Not Fair!
# Home Project

Constant complaining about unfair things may feel good, but it usually does not serve a purpose other than to blow off steam and turn people off. Instead, plan a set hour each week for you and your family to get together and voice complaints. Together, find useful ways for each person to channel his anger. The exercise below will help you learn how to do this.

You are playing touch football with your brothers and sisters and neighborhood friends in your backyard. Your brother Eric, on the opposing team, purposely knocks you down to upset and distract you so that his team can score. You are furious!

What is unfair that makes you angry? _____

Is your anger being directed toward someone who *purposely* wanted to hurt you? _____ If not, is it sensible and useful to be angry at him?

_____

If you know the person purposely wanted to hurt you, what are three ways you could channel your anger productively so that you could reach your desired goal? What is your goal in the situation above?

Example: My goal is to win the game. I will channel my angry energy to play harder and beat the other team.

_____

_____

_____

_____

_____

Your mother was supposed to pick you up early from school so that you could get home to finish a project. You were looking forward to this. She calls to say she'll be at least an hour late because she got stuck with a client at work. You are angry!

What is unfair that makes you angry? _____

Is your anger being directed toward someone who *purposely* wanted to hurt you? _____ If not, is it sensible and useful to be angry at her?

_____

What are at least three ways you could channel your anger productively in order to reach your desired goal? What is your goal in the situation above?
Example: My goal is to work on my project. My mother did not mean to purposely disappoint me. I will use my energy to write ideas for my project in my notebook while I sit and wait for Mom.

_____

_____

_____

# Putt Away Your Anger

Did you ever hear yourself say, "She made me angry." The truth is, other people can't *make* you angry. Play a round of miniature golf and see how your thoughts can create your anger.

Directions: Answer the questions by writing 1, 2, 3, 4 or 5 on your score card. Total your score when you are finished. See how close to par you are. There is a five-stroke limit on all holes. Putt away!

## Phone Call Madness

Your friend does not return your telephone call. You would most likely think:

Hole in 1—I'll try her later.
Hole in 2—She's a real jerk.
Hole in 3—She probably doesn't like me.
Hole in 4—I can't believe she's not calling me back. I can't handle this!
Hole in 5—She's not right. She should always return a phone call.

## Slow as Molasses

The librarian is very slow moving. You have to wait in line a long time just to check out one book. You would most likely think:

Hole in 1—Since I have to wait awhile, I'll start reading my book.
Hole in 2—She's stupid.
Hole in 3—She's doing this to annoy me.
Hole in 4—I'm going to get killed if I get to class late.
Hole in 5—She shouldn't make people wait like this.

Tell your teacher your score. He will explain to you the kinds of thoughts you have that make you more angry or less angry in a situation.

Discuss with your teacher and classmates new thoughts that will cause you less anger.

## Ouch!

Your teacher criticizes you in front of the class. You would most likely think:

Hole in 1—Some of what he said is true. I'd like to change those behaviors.
Hole in 2—He's so mean!
Hole in 3—He probably has a lousy marriage and takes out his anger on me.
Hole in 4—I am totally embarrassed and can never face anyone again.
Hole in 5—He should know better than to yell at me in front of others.

| Scorecard | You | Par |
|---|---|---|
| Phone Call Madness | | 1 |
| Ouch! | | 1 |
| Slow as Molasses | | 1 |
| TOTAL | | 3 |

Cut out your scorecard.

# For the Teacher

**Purposes:** To help students identify the distortions in thinking that intensify angers; to help students learn new thoughts that will reduce their negative emotional reaction.

**Process:** Tell students that they must choose the statement that comes closest to their way of thinking in a given situation. When each student's score is totalled, explain to him the irrational thinking that holes 2-5 describe and how those thoughts generate more anger than the situation calls for. Explain to him that this is what is meant by "creating your own anger." Ask the students to consider more realistic thoughts that would decrease rather than increase their negative emotional reaction to a situation. Keep a classroom chart on the wall. Have the five types of thoughts head each of the five columns. Keep a magic marker next to the chart. Any time one of these statements is said or heard by students, the statement should be written under the column which describes its type. A more realistic statement should be written underneath. Students should begin to be aware and sensitive to irrational thinking. Point out that anger is not good or bad, right or wrong, but that it's not a comfortable emotion to live with. For that reason it can be helpful to learn ways to reduce it.

## Score Card Translations

Hole in 1—If you landed a hole in 1 most often, you are probably a person who is not overwhelmed with angry feelings. You look at a situation for what it is and don't increase your anger by labeling, mind reading, magnifying or moralizing.

Hole in 2—If you landed a hole in 2 most often, you probably *label* when you are angry. Labeling is when you describe the person you are mad at in a completely negative way—"stupid" "idiot" "loser" "wimp." It is true that the person may have hurt you in some way and you may feel resentful or sad or that it wasn't nice of him, but labeling creates him to be *all* bad. He then becomes a target for your anger and this gives way for your need to blame. This intensifies the conflict and the anger.

Hole in 3—If you landed a hole in 3 most often, you probably *mind read* when you are angry. Mind reading means that you invent reasons that explain to your satisfaction why the other person did what he did— "he always has to get his way" or "she's upset because her mother yelled at her." The problem is that they are just misleading labels that are not necessarily true because they haven't been checked by the person you're angry with. Most often the "mind read" thoughts cause both people more anger than the situations call for.

Hole in 4—If you landed a hole in 4 most often, you probably *magnify* when you are angry. Magnifying means you exaggerate the importance of the negative event—"this is going to be the end of the world" or "this is the most horrible thing that could happen to me." Since it is highly improbable that this event will cause the end of the world or that it is the MOST horrible thing that could happen, your emotional reaction gets blown out of proportion. Your anger gets intensified.

Hole in 5—If you landed a hole in 5 most often, you probably use *shoulds* and *shouldn'ts* when you are angry. This means that when other people's actions are not to your liking, you tell yourself they *should or shouldn't* have done what they did. If you insist on perfection from others, you will be frustrated and intensify your anger and conflicts.

Concepts adapted from *Feeling Good*, David Burns, 1980, New American Library.

# For the Parents

Through the Putt Away Your Anger activities, children will learn to reduce their anger in situations by changing irrational thoughts to rational ones. They will understand that changing thoughts changes feelings and that no one can really MAKE one angry but oneself. Try identifying your own irrational thoughts caused by labeling, magnifying, mind reading and using shoulds and shouldn'ts and add pages to the "Cool Down Family Booklet."

# Putt Away Your Anger
# Home Project

Fill in the chart below. Then write the situations, your "cooled down" thoughts with illustrations on separate pieces of drawing paper. Ask family members to write their own situations, "cooled down" thoughts with illustrations and create a family booklet. When family members get heated up, suggest they look through the "Cool Down Family Booklet" for the thoughts that may reduce their negative emotional reactions. Add pages to the booklet whenever heated situations arise.

| Situations | Thoughts That Make My Temperature Rise | Kinds of Thoughts<br>L—labeling<br>M—mind reading<br>Ma—magnifying<br>S—shoulds | Realistic Thoughts That Help Me Cool Down |
|---|---|---|---|
| **Example:** Your sister forgets to return the sweater she borrowed. | "She makes my life miserable. She should always return what she borrows." | "She makes my life miserable" is Ma (magnifying). "She should return what she borrows" is S for (shoulds). | I can't expect my sister to be perfect. I'll remind her again tomorrow. |
| You do all your chores and homework and your mother still won't let you stay overnight at your friend's house. | | | |
| Your parents promise to take you to the circus, but plans have to be cancelled because your father has to work late. | | | |
| Your brother criticizes you for the way you are eating. | | | |

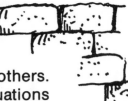

Competing and cooperating occur naturally as you interact with others. The activities in this chapter will help you know appropriate situations in which to compete and cooperate. Used at the right time, your relationships can improve and you can grow to your fullest potential.

### Before You Begin "Cooperation and Competition"

Unscramble the following vocabulary words.

eilmpco _____

traeucca _____

laiicefnbe _____

cumanesctsirc _____

pprpoairtea _____

nocdfincee _____

eegnhlacl _____

Write the definitions below.

appropriate _____

confidence _____

compile _____

challenge _____

circumstances _____

beneficial _____

accurate _____

# Small Word Search

1. As a class, see how many small words (two or more letters) you can find in the big word *cooperation*. Make one long list on the chalkboard. You MUST work together with your classmates to succeed. Good luck! Your teacher will time you. You have only fifteen minutes. On your mark, get set, go!

## COOPERATION

| | | |
|---|---|---|
| _____ | _____ | _____ |
| _____ | _____ | _____ |
| _____ | _____ | _____ |
| _____ | _____ | _____ |
| _____ | _____ | _____ |
| _____ | _____ | _____ |

2. Working alone, see how many small words (two or more letters) you can find in the big word *competition*. Make a long list below. Do not work together with your classmates, but rather see which classmates can find the most words in the fifteen minutes allowed. Good luck! Your teacher will time you. On your mark, get set, go!

## COMPETITION

| | | |
|---|---|---|
| _____ | _____ | _____ |
| _____ | _____ | _____ |
| _____ | _____ | _____ |
| _____ | _____ | _____ |
| _____ | _____ | _____ |
| _____ | _____ | _____ |

3. Answer the following questions after completing 1 and 2. Discuss your answers with your teacher and classmates.
   Write your own definition of *cooperation* after doing #1. Then write the dictionary definition. See how they compare.
   (your definition)_____
   (dictionary definition) _____
   Write your own definition of *competition* after doing #2. Then write the dictionary definition. See how they compare.
   (your definition)_____
   (dictionary definition) _____
   Did you feel better competing or cooperating? Why? _____
   _____
   Did you have more successful results competing or cooperating? Why?
   _____
   What was difficult and what was easy for you when cooperating? What was difficult and what was easy for you when competing?
   _____
   Did you feel closer to your classmates doing one of them? Why? Which?
   _____
   In which did you have more fun? Learn more? Get less frustrated?
   _____

# For the Teacher

**Purposes:** To learn the definitions of *cooperation* and *competition* and make comparisons between the two; to give students the experience of cooperating and competing and of evaluating their feelings in each; to compare the results of each; to develop vocabulary and spelling abilities; to play a word game.

**Process:** Write the word *cooperation* on the board. Ask students what will be necessary, individually and as a group, to complete the task successfully. Make sure they understand the rules. These include raising hands when they see a small word, not naming names, not using a letter more than once in a word (if there is no double of it), and making sure each word is two letters or more. Use a timer and stop after fifteen minutes. Ask the students how they felt cooperating to complete this task and if they imagine they would have more success competing with each other. Find out their reasons and tell them they will have the opportunity to find out in their next activity.

Write the word *competition* on the board. Ask the students what will be necessary to complete the task alone and successfully. Point out the differences in goals between the two. In the first activity, the goal is to work together as a team and find as many words as possible. No one stands out as best and everyone wins. In the second activity, the goal is to find more words than anyone else— to beat, win and be best. Once again, make sure they understand the rules. These include the following: words must be two letters or more, no letters can be used twice and no names are allowed. All words should be listed on their own sheets, and each person's list will be counted and checked by you, the teacher. You will then announce the winner. Use a timer and tell the students to put their pencils down after fifteen minutes. Ask the students how they felt competing to complete the task and how it was similar and different from cooperating. How did they feel with one winner? Did they end up feeling like a loser?

Discuss with the students the answers to their questions listed on the bottom of their activity page.

# For the Parents

Your child will experience the feelings and results of cooperating and competing while becoming more aware of the ways he cooperates and competes at home. Through the Small Word Search activities, he can determine the positive and negative aspects of both and how they help and hinder him in his relations with others and his success in the world. Your child will realize that neither cooperating nor competing is better or worse, right or wrong, but rather more helpful in some situations than in others. These situations will be discussed in some of the following activities.

# Small Word Search
# Home Project

With your family or one other family member, compile a list of all the ways you are COOPERATIVE in the family. Time yourselves. You have only fifteen minutes to come up with as long and accurate a list as possible, together. Good luck! On your mark, get set, go!

## COOPERATIVE

<u>I help with the dishes.</u>

_____    _____    _____

_____    _____    _____

_____    _____    _____

_____    _____    _____

_____    _____    _____

_____    _____    _____

Working alone, compile a list of all the ways you are COMPETITIVE in the family. Ask another family member to compile his own list of all the ways he is COMPETITVE in the family. Do not work together, but rather see who can come up with the longest list in the fifteen minutes allowed. Good luck! Time yourselves. On your mark, get set, go!

## COMPETITIVE

<u>I try to be as good as</u>
<u>my sister in math.</u>

_____    _____    _____

_____    _____    _____

_____    _____    _____

_____    _____    _____

_____    _____    _____

Discuss with your family what is positive about cooperating and competing in the family. Let them know if there is anything about it you would like to change.

Save this exercise to use with the "Which Is What?" home project.

 # Which Is What?

Imagine you've just told your friends about the new stereo system your parents bought you. Put an X over the responses which are competitive ones. If you get tic-tac-toe (in the pattern your teacher will show you), congratulate yourself on knowing the differences between competitive and cooperative statements.

| My parents bought me one before your parents bought you one. | I bet mine sounds much better than yours. Our family buys better quality than yours. | You're so spoiled. You get whatever you want. You'll be sorry one of these days. I'm better than you anyway. |
|---|---|---|
| You are so lucky. I would love to hear it someday, and I'll bring over some records we can both listen to. | That's great! Do you need any help installing it? I'm good at that! I'd be glad to help. | Congratulations. Let me know what tapes you like. I'd like to buy you some. |
| Good. Now maybe I can convince my parents to buy me one. | It must be nice to get whatever you ask for. I have to save my allowance for anything I want. | Now you probably think you're better than the rest of us. It's not true. You're just a wimp so who cares about your stereo. |

Imagine you've just won the lead in the class play. Put an O over the responses that you get from your classmates which are cooperative ones. If you get tic-tac-toe (in the pattern your teacher will show you), congratulate yourself on knowing the differences between competitve and cooperative statements.

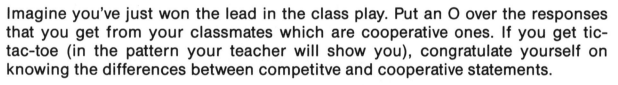

| Congratulations! I would love to help you (if you need me) memorize your lines. Let me know. | You didn't do that much better than anyone else. I think you got it only because you are the teacher's pet. | Even though I tried out for it, I'm glad I didn't get it. Now I realize that I'd hate to be in your shoes. You have so much to practice and learn. |
|---|---|---|
| How about if we all get together tonight and celebrate with you. | I'm better than you in most things. This was just luck that you got the main role. | I'd love to help you get a costume prepared. I have some good ideas. |
| I'd like to take your picture and send it to the school newspaper. | You really deserve the part. You are so talented. I will get lots of people to come the night of the performance. | I am going to complain to the principal. It's not fair because you got a part last year! |

# For the Teacher

**Purposes:** To help students recognize competitve and cooperative responses and to identify their reactions to them.

**Process:** Begin by discussing the meanings of *competitive* and *cooperative* and ask students to give examples of times they've been one way or the other. Point out the differences. Also help them to notice the differences in the way each response makes them feel. Remind the students that neither is good nor bad/right nor wrong necessarily if each is used in the appropriate situations. Explain to them the rules of tic-tac-toe. Write the answer key on the board when they have finished.

Have the students answer and discuss the following questions:

- How do you feel and react if someone is being competitive/cooperative with you? Discuss the situation on the other side.

- What are situations that cause you to be competitive/cooperative with others?

- Are you satisfied with the way you compete? Cooperate?

- Who in your life do you compete most with? Why? Cooperate most with? Why? Are you satisfied with this? What do you want to change about this?

- What is the main difference between competing and cooperating?

- When do you feel OK competing? When do you not feel OK competing?

**Answer Key**

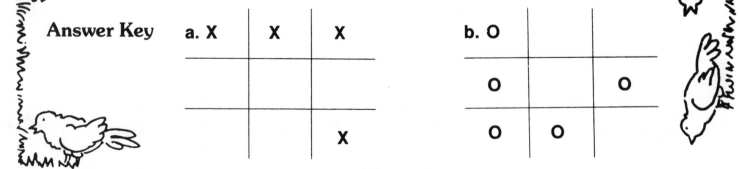

# For the Parents

Which Is What? activities help your child recognize competitive and cooperative statements and identify his feelings and reactions to them. The activities also ask your child to examine his competitive and cooperative ways and to decide which help to improve relations and in which circumstances. It is important for the child to understand that neither cooperating nor competing is necessarily good or bad/right or wrong, if each is used in the appropriate situation. Get to know your child better by playing Which Is What? tic-tac-toe together. Discuss the results and come out winners!

# Which Is What?
# Home Project

Go back to Small Word Search home project. Copy from your lists five ways you are cooperative and four ways competitive in your family. Write each in a box below.

| | | |
|---|---|---|
| | | |
| | | |
| | | |

After you've written each one in a box, draw an X over the ones which help you to get along best with family members. Draw an O over the ones which help you feel good about yourself and others. See if you get tic-tac-toe.

Discuss with family members when competing/cooperating is beneficial to you and to the family relations. Discuss the necessary change if something is not.

# Race to the Finish Line

Read the list below. Decide in which situations and circumstances it would be appropriate to compete and in which it would be appropriate to cooperate. Write the statements under the correct columns. See which list makes it to the finish line.

- Your class can go out to recess only if the classroom gets cleaned up.
- You are campaigning for the position of class president.
- You and your team must come up with an idea for the class trip.
- You would like to make the cheerleading squad. There is only room for two more people.
- You would like to do better than you did last time in the five-mile race.
- Your mother needs help with the groceries and the laundry.
- Your basketball team is playing the championship game.
- Your sister can only complete her assignment if you give her the information you've collected.
- Your friend can only get his class picture taken if you lend him your jacket and tie.
- You would like to be selected for Musician of the Year.
- The best dancer will get the lead in the play.
- You would like to win Best Project in the science fair.

| **Compete** | **Cooperate** |
| --- | --- |
| _____ | _____ |
| _____ | _____ |
| _____ | _____ |
| _____ | _____ |
| _____ | _____ |
| _____ | _____ |
| _____ | _____ |

FINISH LINE!

Discuss with your teacher and classmates when it is beneficial and appropriate to compete and cooperate and why.

# For the Teacher

**Purpose:** To help students determine appropriate situations and circumstances in which to compete and cooperate.

**Process:** Explain to students that there are situations/circumstances when cooperating will be more helpful in reaching a desired goal and other situations/circumstances when competing will be. Point out that cooperating is usually more helpful when each person's contributions will help reach a common end or purpose. Competing, on the other hand, is usually more for the purpose of matching another's skill or ability and vying for position or prize. Using the wrong one at the wrong time can be destructive and rarely helps a person reach a desired goal. Ask students to carefully read the list and decide whether competing or cooperating would be appropriate to the situation. Tell them to write that situation under the correct column.

Have students answer and discuss the following questions:

- Think of at least one situation in which you are competing, but it would be more helpful for you to cooperate.

- Think of at least one situation in which you are cooperating, but it would be more helpful for you to compete.

- What steps will you have to take to reverse these?

# For the Parents

Competing and cooperating can be helpful behaviors if your child uses them at appropriate times and in appropriate situations. Race to the Finish Line activities are designed to help your child recognize which behavior for which situation will help him reach his desired goals. He will also have the opportunity to identify the present situations in his life which could benefit with alternative behaviors. Help your child race to the finish line and reach his desired goals.

# Race to the Finish Line
# Home Project

Decide what would be more helpful and beneficial in each situation and write it below.

Your sister and you are both competing for the front seat in your mother's new car. Your parents warn you that neither of you will go for the ride if the fighting continues.

Is competing the best choice of behavior in this situation? Why or why not? Will it help you reach your goal of sitting in the front seat?

_____

_____

_____

_____

Write a better alternative below.

_____

_____

_____

_____

You are angry because it seems that your parents trust your brother more than you. This makes you compete with him. You refuse to ever help him, you set things up so that he will get in trouble and you start fights with him constantly. Your behavior with your brother makes your parents trust you less.

Is competing the best choice of behavior in this situation? Will it help you to reach your goal of being more trusted by your parents?

_____

_____

_____

_____

Write a better alternative below.

_____

_____

_____

_____

Discuss with your family or a family member other situations at home in which alternative behaviors would be more helpful to you in reaching your goals. Together, decide the alternatives.

# Cut It Out!

We compete for many different reasons. Some are helpful in building our confidence and others are not. Read the reasons below that people choose to compete. Get your scissors. Cut out the boxes which are not helpful to building self-confidence.

| | | |
|---|---|---|
| If the person I compete with loses, that proves to me the truth about myself. It proves that I'm special. | I compete so that I can learn my strengths and abilities. | I compete to show off and show up others. |
| If the person I'm competing with wins, that proves to me the truth about myself. It proves that I'm a loser. | I compete because I enjoy the excitement of testing my limits. | I compete in order to challenge myself to do better and better. |
| I compete to prove to everyone that I'm worthwhile. | The way I know I'm smart is knowing that everyone else is dumber than I am. | I compete to be the best that I can be. |

Discuss with your teacher and classmates the reasons you cut out the boxes that you did. Explain why those reasons for competing would not help to build a person's confidence.

# For the Teacher

**Purpose:** To help students identify reasons for competing that do not usually help a person develop confidence.

**Process:** Explain to students that competing will have negative outcomes if one bases his self-worth on winning or losing or if he uses it to prove he is better or worse than another. Give examples of each and ask students to share their experiences of this. Have them explain, in their own words, why competing worked against them instead of for them.

Have students answer and discuss the following questions:

- Why do you think competing to prove that you are better than anyone else will NOT help you to build confidence? What is a better reason for competing?

- Why do you think believing you are a failure if you lose a competition could lead you to a poor self-image? What would be a more realistic and positive belief?

# For the Parents

Children need to learn that competing will have negative outcomes if they base their self-worth on winning or losing or if competing is used to prove they are better or worse than someone else. Cut It Out activities help your child compare the positive and negative reasons for competing. The activities ask him to identify and give examples of the ways he competes for positive results. Share some of the ways you compete and discuss the outcomes with your child. Tell him if your need to compete has changed over the years and how it was similar to or different from your child's at his age.

# Cut It Out
# Home Project

Listed below are some of the positive reasons for competing. Give examples of what you do or plan to do to compete in these ways.

**I compete because I enjoy the excitement of testing my limits.**

Examples: <u>Every day I try to jump just a little higher than the day before.</u>

_____

_____

_____

_____

_____

**I compete so that I can learn my strengths and abilities.**

Examples: <u>Every time I play tennis with my brother, I develop my backhand.</u>

_____

_____

_____

_____

_____

**I compete to be the best that I can be.**

Examples: <u>I try to study as hard or harder than my sister since she does</u>

<u>so well in her studies.</u>

_____

_____

_____

_____

Tell family members the positive reasons for competing with them.

# The ABC's of Solving Problems

Resolving conflicts and solving problems are helpful skills to learn so that you can get along with others. The activities in this chapter teach effective ways to solve problems and resolve conflicts and help you develop the tools necessary to do both.

## Before You Begin "The ABC's of Solving Problems"

Try to guess what the italicized vocabulary words mean by using context clues. Then look up each word and write the dictionary definition. See how close you come.

It was difficult to *resolve* our problem, because she wouldn't talk.

Guess _____

Dictionary definition _____


We had a *conflict* because I wanted cookies and she wanted candy.

Guess _____

Dictionary definition _____


She had a lot of information about me that she could use as *ammunition*.

Guess _____

Dictionary definition _____


I *defended* my idea because I didn't want to sound stupid.

Guess _____

Dictionary definition _____


I felt *rejected* when he asked me to go home early.

Guess _____

Dictionary definition _____

# Finding a Problem and Solution

Have you ever found yourself fighting with a friend but not knowing what you were really fighting about? In order to resolve a conflict between yourself and another person, you must first know exactly what the problem is that needs to be solved. Read the story and answer the questions below to help you identify the problem between Michelle and Jennifer.

---

"I asked you not to put the alarm clock on to wake you because it gets me up one hour earlier than necessary," yelled Michelle to her sister Jennifer.

"Tough; I told you that I can't wake up without my alarm—there is nothing I can do about it!" shouted Jennifer.

"You get me so mad. You are always thinking just of yourself," cried Michelle.

"That's not true," demanded Jennifer. "I'm always quiet getting ready for school or if I stay up later than you."

"I just don't want that alarm clock ringing anymore at 7:00 in the morning," Michelle insisted.

---

## Problem-Solving Questions

What does Michelle want or need? _____

What does Jennifer want or need? _____

How do their wants (or needs) differ or conflict causing them to have problems?
_____

Do they sound more like they want to:
  ● solve their problems?
  ● fight to release their anger?
  ● prove who is right or wrong?
  ● fight until there is a winner and a loser?
_____

**Remember:**  When people are invested in fighting or arguing in order to get rid of anger, gain control or be the winner, usually a solution to the problem can never be found (since it is not what they are looking for).

If you believe Michelle and Jennifer *want* to find a solution to their problem, read below to see how to solve the conflict.

## Method of Solving Problems

Identifying the problem:

  ● Jennifer needs an alarm to wake up, but Michelle does not want to be disturbed by the alarm clock.

Brainstorm all possible solutions:
(no matter how silly, impossible or ridiculous)

  ● Jennifer has her mother or father wake her.
  ● Michelle sleeps with cotton in her ears.
  ● They take turns sleeping on the couch in the living room.
  ● Jennifer gets a quieter alarm clock.

## Finding a Workable Compromise

Choose the best solution from the list that meets the needs of both people. (Both people vote.)

Example: Jennifer gets a quieter alarm clock.

# For the Teacher

**Purpose:** To help students learn the skills of identifying conflicts and finding workable solutions.

**Process:** Explain to students that a conflict is usually the result of people needing and/or wanting opposing things. In order to resolve a conflict, each person must be clear about what it is he wants or needs and how it clashes with what the other person wants or needs. Point out the differences between fighting (or arguing) for the purposes of winning, controlling, proving worth, being right or for the purpose of solving the problem. Help students to solve their problems by teaching them how to brainstorm *any* solution that comes to mind, no matter how silly or improbable, with the person they are in conflict with. Then teach them to go through each suggested solution and decide if it is a workable compromise for each person involved. Help them discover the best of the possible solutions and ways for each person to put it into practice. Define compromise as a way of settling differences by each side yielding.

Have students answer and discuss the following questions:

- When you have a problem with someone else, do you usually fight, run away, or try to solve the problem? Are you satisfied with the way you deal with a problem? If not, how would you like it changed?

- What do you find easy and most difficult when it comes to conflicts?

# For the Parents

Finding a Problem and Solution activities will help your child know what he is fighting for or about (when he is in conflict with someone else) and learn to find workable solutions to the problem. Your child will learn to use his energy to solve the problem, rather than using it to fight or argue for the purpose of proving himself to the other person. As a result, he will gain confidence and certainly win friends.

# Finding a Problem and Solution
# Home Project

Think of a problem you have with a family member in which you want something which conflicts with what the other person wants. Write the problem and the problem-solving questions on the input card and enter them in your computer. Write the results on the printout sheet below.

## Input Card

Problem: _____

_____

### Problem-Solving Questions:

- What do I want?
- What does the other person want?
- How do our wants conflict?
- Do we each really want to solve the problem or do we each prefer just to fight?

## Printout Sheet

All possible solutions:

_____

_____

_____

_____

_____

_____

_____

Best solution for both of us:

_____

_____

_____

# Blast Off!

A problem can best be solved through discussion rather than argument. Decide which statements in the rocket ships would help get a discussion off the ground and color those rockets' flames red. Read the definitions of *discussion* and *arguing* below before coloring the flames.

Why can't you ever be on time?

Don't be so unfair about it!

Are you saying that you don't want me to be so loud?

I need you to call me if you are going to be late.

I don't want to talk about it.

You should have known better!

It wasn't my fault. I tried.

When you asked me to clean the kitchen, I felt bad.

*Discussion* is an exchange of ideas, feelings, thoughts and opinions. It is relating to one another. It makes for better understanding and problem solving.

*Arguing* is avoiding one another. Its purpose is also to express ideas, feelings, thoughts and opinions but with the purpose of insulting and hurting others. It stops problem solving and creates anger.

Compare the statements that would get a discussion off the ground with those that would keep the discussion from going anywhere (except lead to arguments and explosions). Discuss with your teacher and classmates the differences between the statements.

# For the Teacher

**Purposes:** To identify the differences between statements that lead to discussions and problem solving and those that lead to arguments; to help students learn the different purposes of discussions and arguments.

**Process:** Explain to students that discussions help to solve problems, and arguments hinder problem solving. The words chosen to communicate feelings can make the difference between starting an argument or a discussion. Each has a different purpose or motivation.

Write on the board and discuss with your class the difference between types of statements that start discussions and lead to resolving differences and the statements that start arguments and block resolving differences.

## Types of Statements That Start Discussions

### "I Want " statements:

"I want you to help me."

"I want to be able to spend more time with you."

These are direct statements which may bring about the desired result.

### "I Feel" statements:

"I feel embarrassed when you tease me."

"When you told me your thoughts, I felt good."

These statements express emotion and tell the other person information about oneself (without blaming).

### "Reflection" statements:

"It sounds like I made you sad."

"Would you prefer if I leave you alone?"

These statements confirm that we have understood the message sent to us. It encourages listening and a response.

### "Telling About Ourselves" statements:

"I wasn't listening when you were telling about your sister."

"I'm afraid of the dark and that's why I said no to you."

These statements are open, honest and sincere and help people know each other better.

## Types of Statements That Start Arguments

### "Cutting Off Communication" statements

"Stop this conversation. I want to have fun!"

"Leave me alone already."

These statements purposely cut off discussion and can arouse anger.

### "Insulting Questions" statements:

"Why can't you ever do anything right?

"Don't you know anything?"

These statements invite a defensive response and stop people from getting to know each other.

### "Meaningless" statements:

"You are so cold."

"You are always unfair."

It is not helpful to criticize behavior without being specific as to the problem.

### "You Must" statements:

"You should have told me."

"You must never do that to us."

These statements are bossy and cause fighting, guilt and fear.

# For the Parents

Solving problems is possible through discussions. The words and tone of voice used to express feelings, thoughts and opinions can make the difference between a child starting an argument or a discussion or getting hooked into one. Blast Off activities will help your child choose the words that will promote discussion and open the doors to resolving conflicts.

# Blast Off!
# ᐱᐱᐱᐱᐱᐱᐱᐱᐱᐱᐱᐱᐱᐱᐱᐱᐱᐱᐱ Home Project ᐱᐱᐱᐱᐱᐱᐱᐱᐱᐱᐱᐱᐱᐱᐱᐱᐱᐱᐱ

You must want to start discussions rather than arguments, but what if someone insists on starting arguments with you? You could argue or run away, or you could learn the secret *blast off* method to not getting hooked into arguments. This method helps you calm the other person. Then he is ready to resolve the conflict instead of arguing to prove himself right (causing more conflicts). Read the dialogue below to see how the *blast off* method works.

**Scott:** You always mess me up when I'm working.

**Jake:** It's possible that I mess you up. Would you tell me exactly the ways in which you feel I mess you up?

**Scott:** You are just a loser. Other kids think so, too.

**Jake:** I'm not always a winner, that's for sure, and I'm sure you are right that I'm not looked up to by all the kids. I would still like to know how I mess you up.

**Scott:** You are just stupid.

**Jake:** There are lots of kids smarter than me. I agree with you that I'm not the smartest person in the world. If I know the ways in which you feel I mess you up when you're working, maybe I could change my behavior so you won't feel annoyed with me. I see my behavior really upsets you.

Jake used the *blast off* method. Instead of arguing with Scott or defending himself, he found some way to agree with him (even if Scott's comments were incorrect). He then asked him specific questions to find out exactly what he meant by the criticisms. Once he gets the answers, they will be ready to brainstorm solutions and find a compromise to resolve the conflict. This method will get the arguer off your back because the questions stop him from rejecting you completely and make it possible to get to the problem that has to be solved. By agreeing with him, he eventually runs out of ammunition and will be in a better mood to communicate.

**Write your own script using the *blast off* method.**

Sharon: You *never* do your share of the chores.

You: _____

Sharon: You are just a big baby who always gets Mom on your side.

You: _____

Sharon: Why do I have to have a sister who is such a spoiled brat?

You: _____

Sharon: Why don't you grow up already?

You: _____

Sharon: _____

You: _____

Sharon: _____

You: _____

Read your script to a family member and discuss the ways in which the *blast off* method can be effective in solving problems.

# From Conflicts to Compromise

Think of the big or little conflicts or problems you face every day. Your alarm doesn't go off, your teacher tells you you can't go out for recess, your friend won't let you play in the game, you don't have enough money to buy your favorite t-shirt or you miss the bus. (Hopefully, they all don't happen on the same day!) Now imagine a day in which you don't have *one* conflict or problem with anybody or anything. Write a story about your fantasy day starting from the moment you wake up until the time you go to sleep. Draw pictures to go with your story.

Share your fantasy story with your teacher and classmates.

# For the Teacher

**Purposes:** To help students use their imaginations and improve their writing skills; to help students see that to be problem-free is a fantasy (unrealistic) and learning how to deal with conflict effectively is a reality.

**Process:** Set the scene by asking students to brainstorm a list of all the big and little conflicts and problems that they face daily. Ask them what changes it would take to be problem-free, how realistic it is and how they'd imagine it to feel. Before they begin writing their fantasy day, tell them to choose a setting and write their stories around a typical day (just without the typical problems and conflicts). Point out that it is unrealistic to expect a day to be *completely* free from conflicts or problems—to expect it can lead to frustration and disappointment. It is a more realistic expectation to learn to effectively deal with the conflicts that occur daily. Mention, however, that *expecting* conflict can also lead to it. Rather than *expecting* problems, expect to be able to handle them if and when they arise. Explain to the students that the fun and purpose of this activity is to have the chance to fantasize being conflict-free for a day. After the students have written and illustrated their stories, ask them to read them to the class. Discuss with them ways they could reduce the number of conflicts they typically experience and/or find effective ways to deal with them. Compile each student's story (tear the pages out of the workbook) into a large class booklet. Tell students to read or reread the book when they are feeling overwhelmed and need an escape.

Have the students answer and discuss the following questions:

● What's OK about having conflicts? What's not OK?

● What can you learn from having conflicts and problems? Does it mean that there is something *wrong* with you if you have conflicts and problems? Explain.

● What has been the most effective way for you to resolve conflicts?

# For the Parents

Learning how to make compromises is the most effective way to resolve most conflicts. From Conflicts to Compromise activities give children the practice of finding compromises for various kinds of conflicts. Together with your child, find creative compromises to the conflicts that occur in the family. Put these compromises into action.

# From Conflicts to Compromise
# Home Project

Since a day without conflicts or problems is unlikely, practice and learn the skill of making compromises, in order to resolve conflicts, when they do arise. Find compromises to resolve the conflicts in the situations below. Remember a compromise means settling differences by each side giving up something.

1. Your mother wants you to wash the dishes now. You want to catch the end of your favorite program now.

   Compromise _____

2. Your brother wants the light off in the bedroom you share, since he wants to go to sleep. You want the light on, since you must finish your homework.

   Compromise _____

3. Your sister wants to have some of your Halloween candy since she did not go trick or treating. You promised two of your friends you'd share it with them. There's not enough for everyone.

   Compromise _____

4. You want to play in the softball game that your brother is managing. He won't let you since he already has even teams.

   Compromise _____

Discuss with your family compromises that could help to resolve conflicts at home. Put these compromises into action!

90

# ✱ Blossoming ✱

As you learn how to get along with others successfully, you will grow tall, blossom fully, branch in new and positive directions and leave to fall your old, ineffective ways of relating.

On the branches of the tree below, write the new directions you would like your interactions to take. (I would like to compete less with my friends and be more helpful.) On the leaves that have fallen to the ground, write the ways you've interacted in the past that have not enhanced your relationships and you want to let go of. (I want to let go of arguing so much with others.) On the leaves on the branches, write the qualities you possess that enable you to have good relationships. (I am very sensitive.) On the buds that are blossoming, write the names of the people you love and love you. Color the tree, its branches and leaves.

91

Although this ends *Interactions*, hopefully the book has planted the seeds that will help you begin or continue to have loving, nurturing relationships with others.